The
Higher-
Consciousness
— Approach to —
Forgiveness

Felicity Nicole

First published in 2025 by Onyx Publishing, an imprint of Notebook Group Limited, 11 Arden House, Deepdale Business Park, Bakewell, Derbyshire, DE45 1GT.

www.onyxpublishing.com
ISBN: 9781913206772

A CIP catalogue record for this book is available from the British Library.

Typeset by Onyx Publishing of Notebook Group Limited.

ONYX PUBLISHING

If you've already read my first book, *Pieces of Me*, then you already know how challenging my relationships with my first husband and my birth family have been. My personal pursuit of peace and contentment has been a long-winded journey, and it took me a long time to understand how integral forgiveness was to this goal. In the summer of 2023, right in the middle of the release of *Pieces of Me*, this fully clicked for me. It felt as if God had removed a veil that had been clouding my vision during my journey and replaced it with complete clarity. We will start this story there.

This book is dedicated to my son, Evan—my All-Star. You make me proud every day as a mother. Most importantly, I dedicate this book to myself, for finally choosing me, for having the courage to rebuild my life on my own terms and vision. And to all the women who haven't yet put themselves first—may this be your time.

1

The Difficulty of Forgiveness

————

THE SUMMER OF 2023 WAS a wild time for me. I was scheduled to have my gallbladder removed that June, and to top things off, I was feeling really agitated with everyone and everything.

You'd have thought I'd have been full of joy at this point in my life, what with my book release and *Pieces of Me* quickly hitting the international bestseller list. But truth be told, God was testing me so I could elevate and understand the depths of my own capacity for forgiveness. My spiritual journey was just beginning... again. I didn't know this at the time, though. In fact, I had done so much personal growth and development over the past few years that my near-constant state of agitation and unease was a little baffling to me. I felt stumped. What was I still not understanding here? Why, after all my healing work, was I still nowhere near the state of peace I wanted to be in? Why was I still so easily triggered?

One week after a particularly triggering incident at my son's recent baseball game, I was sitting in a meditation when it hit me right in the face. At the time, I had been reading *Mary Magdalene Revealed* by Meggan Watterson, and in my state of meditation, I received a message direct from Mary: *You still are not speaking your truth.*

I had to write that down immediately and think about it later. What was Mary referring to?

In *Mary Magdalene Revealed*, Watterson cautions against any connection to the seven deadly sins (wrath, gluttony, greed, lust, sloth, pride, and envy). Sure enough, I could see that the emotional dysregulation I'd experienced at my son's baseball game was just me projecting my near-constant underlying feelings of wrath (which is just anger) onto anything in sight. I had used the baseball game as a scapegoat.

Why had I been angry in the first place? Because (as Mary pointed out) I was still not speaking or living in my truth. I was still holding onto a ton of old resentment from my marital relationship and abandonment issues. And I had taken it all out on my son's baseball team. (T.T., I am truly sorry for all the emails I sent during that time. I hold myself fully accountable for being a Karen!)

I would need to dig deep and pray hard to let this resentment go; to move up.

There were many (understandable, I think) reasons why I was still harboring so much resentment at this point in my healing journey. More on that shortly. For now, so what if my son's travel ball team was a total shitshow? This was no longer my problem anyway: my husband, John, had, for the first time and after noticing my stress, stepped up to the plate and taken over managing travel ball for me. Talk about a gift from God! Not only did this lead to Evan's team having some amazing wins (and Evan's batting average going through the roof), but it also meant I now had some time to focus on my book release, the creation of *She Is You* (my magazine), and all the fun stuff my PR firm had me doing.

While this felt like a blessing at the time—my schedule was full, in a way that I loved—it meant that my journey of learning how to speak my truth (and exploring my odd newfound connection to Mary Magdalene) would need to go on the back burner for now. I was on my way up, and fast.

One night during this period, I was hit at 2AM with what I thought were heart attack symptoms. I awoke with my chest in intense pain. I took a breath and tried to roll over to the other side of the bed, and holy shit: the pain began to radiate down my left arm. I could barely breathe because of the sheer intensity, let alone speak.

By this time, John and I were sleeping in separate bedrooms. The stubborn old man had taken the bougie first-floor master, while I had taken residence upstairs, on the second-floor master. Now, as I writhed around in pain, I was kind of wishing we'd stayed in the same bedroom. I grabbed my phone (and my dog, Charlie) and scooted down the stairs to the main floor. I struggled to speak because of the pain, but I was able to yelp out, "John!"

No response.

"John!"

No response.

A third time: "John!"

Still no response.

I dialed 911. Just as the operator answered, John emerged from his bedroom to find me on the foyer floor, sliding the phone toward his feet and yelping out, "Heart attack! Heart attack!" He clicked, and before I knew it, I had eight paramedics at my home shoving aspirin down my throat and taking my vitals as I yowled out in pain. My chest hurt so bad. Like, catastrophically bad.

This is where I get deep into the spiritual stuff:

In the weeks leading up to this, I'd been having intense dreams that reflected my need for better protection. Many people had not wanted *Pieces of Me* to be released or my story to be told, and I'd heard through the grapevine that my sister Dawn had been voicing some not-so-kind opinions of me. This toxic energy was being pushed toward me and (in my opinion) was manifesting into heart attack symptoms. (This is one of the gifts that God has given me as an empath: the ability to feel and work through conflict in my dreams.) Suffice it to say, I hadn't heeded the warnings my dreams had very clearly been sending me. This is because I had been going through somewhat of a spiritual crisis. I wasn't sure how to make use of my spiritual gifts (including my clairvoyant dreams) without disrespecting my Catholic foundations. So, there John and I were, in the emergency room. This felt like my twentieth visit in the past two years.

By the time the doctor walked in, I'd had all the preliminary tests done and had been cleared of a heart attack. So, what was going on? The doc suggested a CT, which showed I had pancreatitis. Pancreatitis! I was far from a classic case of this. I pointed this out, and the doctor responded, "Yes, but we think it's due to your medication."

I thought, *That damn Mounjaro! Fuck.* I loved it because it curbed my appetite and helped my insulin resistance. Even with all my fasting and discipline, I was still insulin-sensitive enough that my doctor thought the lowest dose would help my body break down my insulin. A possible side effect of this, however, was pancreatitis.

Goodbye, Mounjaro. Back to hardcore discipline and clear liquids until I could see the surgeon.

Upon performing an ultrasound, we found gallstones, and I was told I needed to be scheduled for surgery. I was sent home to rest and told to stay on a clear diet until I met with my surgeon.

So long, freedom summer. Here I was, in pain and in bed, recovering from something once again. Every cloud has a silver lining, though. This is when all the magic began. This is when I started to fully understand the message I'd received from Mary Magdalene. First, though, I'd need to understand how and why these issues had entered my body in the first place.

The Emotional and Psychological Impact of Unhealed Trauma

A person who has been abused and battered their entire life carries emotional pain deep within their body, including their spiritual body (the chakra system, soul, and aura), throughout their life. The spiritual body, after being abused and battered, resembles a dog who has been left outside its entire life, chained up in the cold with barely any food or water and no love or attention. A person with such a background will subconsciously continue to be guarded because of all the resentment that sits deep in their bones. They will hold onto their "soul story". When you think about trauma in this way, it makes sense that the shame, guilt, abandonment, and broken promises that had filled my spiritual body up until the point of me getting pancreatitis were eating away at me like a demon. Emotional baggage creates an imbalance in energetic flow and ultimately causes a laundry list of physical symptoms, such as Crohn's disease, IBS, high blood pressure, diverticulitis, and any type of autoimmune-related issue in general.

But wait. There is more complexity to this.

If or when we begin to peel back the layers of our trauma and to instead pursue forgiveness, we first need to recognize that the trauma that has been stored inside us isn't just the trauma we've experienced from this lifetime. The trauma goes back seven generations. We hold onto our ancestors' baggage, as *well* as our own. Now doesn't that fucking suck?! Not only am I dealing with my own deep-seated trauma, but I also have to deal with my *ancestors'* trauma? And that's not all: we also hold onto the baggage from *our other lifetimes.*

When I learned this shortly after my pancreatitis recovery, I started to wonder whether there was a connection between Mary Magdalene's message to me ("You are still not speaking your truth") and this discovery. Curious, I started going back to my many different lifetimes through meditation. In some of these lifetimes, I was a child; others, a woman being chased in the woods. Often, I was the target of a witch hunt (many witch hunts, in fact), and in several, I was Joan of Arc herself. I was also taken back to seven different lifetimes in which I was a little girl of Hispanic descent who was battered and abused sexually.

These meditations resonated with me like no others had before.

I refer to this monumental moment of meditational practice as the "golden thread in our lives". Such discoveries feel like a hypnosis journey or an ayahuasca trip. If you can surrender to them and allow them to take you where they want to, past life meditations can help you to recognize the parts that these past lives play in your life today. I have walked a few of my clients through lifetime after lifetime to help them connect the dots of how these lifetimes affect their world today, and their discoveries have been nothing short of incredible.

If you can't or won't go through this journey or face the pain that is lying dormant within you, your physical and emotional self will forever be held hostage to your unhealed trauma. This explained my pancreatitis. I hadn't explored these lifetimes before, which meant I was still harboring the trauma from them, which meant I couldn't live my truth. It also explained why I felt stuck whenever I thought about my spiritual gifts.

Before I had all these realizations and while I was in the aftermath of my pancreatitis situation, I was at baseball practice in the South Side when I recognized Dr. Lisa, a traditional Chinese medicine (TCM) doctor. Her office was around the corner. *Bingo*, I thought. *Talk about divine intervention.* Everyone in the Chicago area who is into alternative medicine goes to her. She is well known and widely respected, and we took my father to her for years. Eager to speak with her, I dropped Evan off at baseball and John and I immediately drove over to her practice.

Dr. Lisa took me in on a walk-in basis right before they closed. I told her what was happening, and she grabbed my wrist to feel my pulse. I knew I was holding onto something; I just wasn't sure what. Obviously, I never thought this lady would be able to pick up on it just by holding my wrist, but that's exactly what happened. Within a few minutes, she blurted out, "You hold onto anger. Your liver and heart are weak. If you don't let this go, you might become physically ill."

Of course, she was correct. I had only just recovered from pancreatitis. I said so, and she prepared six packages of herbs' wood—weeds, too—that I was supposed to drink for six days straight with one day off, and repeat, until the supply was finished. (Side note: It's fascinating to me that TCM treats liver and gallbladder issues through the elements of wood and acupuncture. These treatments help support the body's healing process until you are ready to deal with the emotional part of your suffering, which is pretty cool, if you ask me.)

Thanks to Dr. Lisa, I'd had one breakthrough. I needed to peel the layers off this onion more, though. This time, I called upon God and asked that He help me to understand my purpose with my gifts and to heal on a deeper level, so I could journey deeper into my past and see who was actually holding onto this anger. Sure enough, in a meditation shortly after that, by the beautiful waters of Mexico, I came across a ten-year-old—one of the seven girls I had been in my past lives—who lived on a farm and had been abused her whole life. In this meditation, I discovered she had a bull who she would talk to and pet on the head whenever she needed comfort. The intense eyes of this bull (which stared right at me) sent chills all through my body. I believed this little girl (me) could communicate with this bull and that the bull was her protector, or spirit animal.

Around this time, while I was working with Dr. Lisa and recovering from my surgery, I thought, *Why not pick up a job?* As if there wasn't already enough on my plate! Still, I was craving a change of scene, big time, so I started a position at a furniture store, to get me out of the house. I have a design degree, and I needed to be with people, so why not?

During my one-month stay (yes, only one month, because my release of *Pieces of Me* took off faster than expected), I would walk the aisles each morning fluffing pillows and examining the new pieces. One day, jumping out at me was a beautiful, strong bull painting. The bull looked at me with deep wisdom in her eyes (and yes, she's a she. She told me that), and I couldn't take my eyes off her. Each time I came into the store, I asked (with some worry) whether she had been sold.

Why was I so drawn to this bull? More to the point, why had I chosen to go to work in *that* specific furniture store right after that meditation featuring the little girl and the bull? Had this been divinely guided for a specific reason?

Every Thursday through Sunday, there she hung on that wall, staring at me with those deep, intense eyes, just like the ones I'd seen in my meditation. I finally couldn't resist the temptation or intuitive nudge from my ten-year-old past-life inner child: I brought her home and hung her next to a painting a friend had created of my seven inner children. As soon as I finished hanging the picture and took a step back, I was flooded with images of the little girl from my meditation petting the head of that specific bull. This was her security; her safety. She had cried to this bull. No, scratch that: this had been *my* security and safety. *I* had cried to this bull.

Whenever those seven little girls would look up to me with curiosity and uncertainty during my later meditations, I would embrace them with the words, "It stops here. There will no longer be abuse." I prayed to God to show me the path to forgiveness, and there she was: Mary Magdalene.

But why?

I had to pick up a few books to understand the significance of her arrival in my spiritual journey. As I learned more about her teachings and philosophy, I realized she was the perfect teacher for me on this path to a higher-consciousness approach to forgiveness. I began this journey by meditating on my heart center. I realized this chakra was heavy, dark, and sad, but I could feel and see there was a light way far behind all that pain. "How do I get there?" was the question. It felt a million miles away. Still, I didn't give up. Each day, my spiritual practice took me into the depths of my soul, with Mary guiding me. I homed in on my heart chakra, sending it love. I would say out loud, "I love you, I love, I love," until I could push past all that pain and transmute it into love.

Much like mine, your journey toward forgiveness may be hard and challenging, but it will strengthen you and empower you with courage you never imagined you had. It will also greatly deepen your relationship with God. Embracing your spirituality and a higher-consciousness approach to forgiveness means standing up for yourself and all your inner children. It means breaking generational cycles in favor of self-love.

I believe you are a woman who is willing to venture as deeply as I have into letting go of all your past traumas. Even still, before we begin, you need to cement this decision. Will you stop when the pain gets too intense, or will you persevere? How do you feel about the possibility that through this journey, you will realize that some members of your circle (whether your family, friends, or partner) are incredibly toxic and evil? Deciding in advance how far you are willing to go in your forgiveness journey takes a lot of courage and sacrifice, but it is a necessity if you are to fully embody a higher-consciousness approach to forgiveness.

Have you set your intentions? Good! Let's move on.

W HEN I WAS VENTURING DEEP into the forgiveness aspect of my healing journey (and was therefore regularly researching the concept of forgiveness), I discovered an interest in the cultural or social norms, beliefs, or expectations that may influence an individual's ability or willingness to forgive. After all, these factors play a huge role in shaping one's understanding of forgiveness. They can create added emotional challenges or barriers, or they can help support the quest for emotional freedom. In other words, cultural and societal factors play a significant role in shaping an individual's *capacity* for and *attitude* toward forgiveness. For example, in cultures that emphasize collective identity and interconnectedness, forgiveness is highly valued and viewed as a means to maintain harmony and social cohesion. Meanwhile, justice and retribution take precedence in cultures that prioritize individuality. In the latter case, forgiveness may be seen as a personal choice rather than a societal expectation. Either way, understanding the influence of cultural, religious, and social factors on forgiveness can promote empathy and a broader perspective when we meet individuals from different cultural backgrounds. This knowledge reminds us that forgiveness is a complex and multifaceted phenomenon shaped by many external influences dating back to the birth of man.

It is important to note that cultural and social factors are not deterministic, and that individuals within a given culture or society can still have unique approaches to forgiveness, due to their personal experiences, temperaments, and values. Plus, interpretations of forgiveness within cultures and religions can vary among people and communities (though there are almost always underlying common themes of compassion, healing, and maintaining beneficial relationship dynamics).

The desire to conform to societal expectations, or the fear of being judged, may lead certain people to adopt strong attitudes for or against forgiveness. For example, in my teenage son's world of peer influence, he is encouraged to hold grudges (though I am glad to say that in the end, the goodness of his heart usually prevails, and he forgives). Furthermore, societies that have endured systemic conflict, violence, or oppression may find forgiveness more challenging, as events like these leave deep-rooted generational pain and trauma on entire populations. Wars or injustices can create a collective memory that influences how that society perceives and practices forgiveness.

Let's look at what's going on currently (as I write, in 2024) between Russia and Ukraine to illustrate. If you were a Ukrainian citizen, would you be able to forgive Russia, as a country? If a soldier bombs a church, killing all but one family member, do you think that one family member could (or should) rise in their higher power and forgive?

Social factors, including family dynamics, peer influence, and societal expectations, also affect one's capacity for forgiveness. Upbringing and the quality of the relationships within the family unit particularly play a huge role. A family environment that promotes forgiveness and conflict resolution can foster a greater capacity for forgiveness in later life, while an upbringing where dysfunction and unhealthy behavior is modeled will certainly lead to difficulties in conflict resolution later down the line.

Religion also plays a huge role in attitudes toward forgiveness. In Islam, forgiveness is a fundamental principle. Believers are encouraged to seek forgiveness from Allah and to forgive others, and are taught that forgiveness is an act of mercy and a way to reach spiritual purification. This is incredibly similar to how forgiveness is viewed in eastern philosophy (more on that in a moment) and certain forms of Catholicism. In fact, there's a Catholic prayer ritual that dates back centuries called hesychasm, during which one sits on a stool with their head pushed into their heart and chants a specific *om*, to connect to their heart; to the center of their being; to the eyes of their soul. Some Native American tribes meanwhile emphasize restoring harmony and balance within the community, and forgiveness is therefore a communal act (rituals and ceremonies for reconciliation and healing are often conducted). On the other hand, forgiveness is seen as a personal choice and a means of personal healing in many western cultures; as a way to release negative emotions, promote reconciliation, and restore relationships. In this context, forgiveness is often associated with letting go of resentment and moving forward. In eastern cultures (such as those influenced by Buddhism and Hinduism), forgiveness is viewed as an essential virtue and a path to spiritual enlightenment. Compassion, empathy, and the acceptance of suffering is emphasized, and forgiveness is seen as a means of breaking free from the cycle of karma and reaching inner peace. (You may notice that there are a lot of similarities between Christ's teachings and this outlook.)

Speaking of karma...

Forgiveness and Karma

The term "karma" is almost always used in the incorrect context, as a (not-so-)polite way to say, "I hope they get what they deserve." On the contrary, karma is not about divine punishment. It is the law of cause and effect. It is the idea that every action generates karma that eventually manifests as a result. This means that when we hold onto anger and resentment, or when we seek revenge, we create negative karma that perpetuates suffering and the cycle of hurt. Therefore, to break free from negative karma, grudges, and resentments, the desire for revenge must be released. In this way, the chain of harmful actions and their consequences can be broken.

Think of grudges and resentment like an extension cord that has been plugged into the person who hurt you. They are going to continue sucking energy from you, until the cord is cut and you forgive them. Similarly, forgiving *yourself* is a way of acknowledging mistakes, taking responsibility, and seeking growth. It is a way of liberating yourself from negative karma and allowing for personal transformation.

Do you see the bigger picture here? We are trying to set ourselves free so we can cultivate positive karma and open our hearts to Christ's message.

Forgiveness (in the context of karma) is not solely about avoiding negative consequences. It is also about cultivating positive karma. By forgiving others and ourselves, we generate positive energy and sow the seeds for future positive outcomes. Acts of forgiveness therefore contribute to a harmonious and compassionate mindset, fostering positive interactions and a cycle of virtuous action. Furthermore, true forgiveness entails far more than merely accepting an apology. It means transcending the ego and its attachment to its grievances. It means recognizing the interconnectedness of all beings and realizing that holding onto anger or seeking revenge only perpetuates suffering. By forgiving, we move beyond self-centeredness and cultivate a broader perspective of compassion and empathy. We ultimately recognize that the grudges we're holding onto are not really about us (the "soul") but are more about the ego, and that we therefore need to go through an ego death in order to fully find forgiveness. Forgiveness is humbling for the ego, and it allows the soul to be elevated to the next level of higher consciousness.

———

T HE CONCEPT OF EGO DEATH tends to be explained in rather abstract and theoretical terms. I personally feel it's hard to take any lesson to heart when it's taught this way. So, let me bring the idea of ego death to vivid clarity for you by sharing a story about a time in my life which was very challenging but hugely transformative for me. (We'll also be digging deeper into this chain of events in subsequent chapters.) It started like this:

I was pressed against the cabinet as Jack unraveled me with a deep kiss. Shivers went down my spine as our embrace deepened. My physical self was in ecstasy. My mind was another matter. This affair was an outlet; a distraction. I was avoiding some hardcore shit, and my ego was *very* much in the driving seat.

Jack would be the person to force me to realize that I was seeking peace and forgiveness through external outlets. I was using distractions so I could mask the internal pain that I did not want to deal with. You see, I had not yet found forgiveness in my heart, or the love that I needed to give myself. So I was dissociating through a false story—the story that I was not getting the emotional intimacy I needed from my husband, John, and that I therefore needed to find this intimacy elsewhere. In reality, the problem did not lie with John. I, in fact, was the problem, I had yet to learn how to love myself, and would curtail to an upcoming 2024 winter of me hibernating in my second home/office to really sit in the uncomfortable to understand and embrace the love that I was needing to provide for myself.

In the end, I walked away from that situation in tears. Surprise, surprise. I thanked Jack for our brief friendship (if you would call it that) and watched him walk into the distance as I sat there picking up the pieces of me that were scattered all over the floor yet again. I was a hot mess, and I was most definitely not living in my truth (much like Mary has warned me).

When I got home after this breakup, I grabbed my journal and began to dump the emotions I was feeling; what Jack had made me feel. My ego screamed in protest, but I didn't care. Enough was enough. I had to push my surface-level, ego-based feelings to the side—the ones that were telling me to run back to Jack—and connect with what was going on deep down; with what was actually happening inside me, spiritually and neurochemically, when I connected with Jack. As I scribbled away in my journal, my immediate emotional dump read, *Betrayal, hurt, rejection, fear, sadness, always second best, never first pick.*

Fuck. What had I been doing? How far I had gone in my own self-sabotage was ridiculous.

I dove back into freeform scribbling, and this yielded another disjointed, distressed journal entry: *Jack makes me feel… desired, beautiful, successful, powerful, seen, heard, wanted.*

I had a lot of work to do.

While all of this was going down, I was also suffering with the symptoms of continued undiagnosed illness. I had been dealing with these symptoms for five years by this point, and I was constantly attending a wearying stream of doctor appointments.

I was stuck in a state of disconnect from my family and myself, mind, body, and spirit. It felt like there was always a knot in my stomach that would sometimes drift to my chest. (This makes sense; my solar plexus and heart chakra were blocked.)

As things skyrocketed in my business, I only felt more and more distanced from everyone and everything I loved. I ended up hiring help in my home because my body was literally breaking down on me. I had zero energy to care for my family, let alone examine the road of self-betrayal I'd gone down during the affairs.

I was also dealing with severe insomnia, probably triggered by my CPTSD (complex posttraumatic stress disorder). I was heavily sedating myself with clonazepam and temazepam at night, yet I was *still* not sleeping. The demands of my magazine, my interviews for *Pieces of Me*, and my chronic illness were wreaking havoc on my mind and body.

Finally, I was diagnosed with gastroparesis (stomach paralysis). Let me tell you, stomach paralysis is not fun. Nothing wants to go in or out. I was a walking time bomb with all the laxatives I had to take (lovely, I know). On top of this (as if this wasn't enough), I had also become seriously anemic. I immediately gained twenty pounds through the gastroparesis, and this only worsened my already-miserable state. There was no time to process and hibernate, though: I had a television interview scheduled right after I received my diagnosis. My doc loaded me up on meds just so I could make my appearance and not have to worry about me puking or shitting my pants on air (hot, fellas, am I right?).

My saving grace during this time was my best friend, Will. I could always be upfront and honest with him when he checked in on me to see how I was feeling. Still, one day, I could feel depression creeping in, foreboding and certain like a hurricane. Then, boom: it was here in full force.

On the outside looking in, everything in my life seemed to be going amazingly well. I was just about to peak, professionally speaking, when my breakdown came. I pled with my psychiatrist to allow me to go to one more event before I went on a work hiatus, so I could tie up all loose ends in my professional life and then not feel guilty about halting production on everything (except the mag) so I could start seriously healing. This was a great speaking opportunity that I just couldn't miss (though I was so seriously sick that I would have just canceled if it weren't for my internal Gen X work ethic: *suck it up, buttercup, and deal with it*). My psychiatrist agreed, so I went and found a big puffy spring dress that would allow me to wear a diaper discreetly (the laxatives, remember?) and I hit the road.

The event was a sellout. I rocked it. My PR rep was in touch with me pretty much straight away to pass on a message from the network: they wanted more.

This didn't exactly fit into my plan for a work hiatus, so I asked them to give me a few days to consider, and I spoke to God: "Okay, Papa, you have full reign over my everything. You have my full surrender. Take over, please." It was then that I fell into an insanely busy work period. We had our spring/summer magazine printed (all one thousand five hundred copies needed to be mailed out, stat), I already had writers working on the fall/winter copy, and I had a ton of TV interviews lined up. Still, my health wasn't improving, and I really needed that break. I had a call with my PR firm so I could give them this update on my health and communicate that I needed a hiatus from podcasts and interviews, so I could slow down and get the last issue of *She Is You* out. They agreed, and we postponed everything until the following fall, except the mags. We cranked those out and mailed them, and also got the mag's schedule in order for the next issue.

Done. Surely *now* I could go on my work break.

Not so fast: I was asked to (and I agreed to) continue re-recording the audio of *Pieces of Me* and follow through on the documentary. These tasks didn't seem too taxing. Still, it wasn't the work break I'd desperately needed.

During this time, one of my friends, Jess, was in my kitchen washing her hands when she looked up at me and said, "You know what, Felicity? You did it. You said you were going to publish a book, and you did. And you took your brand from blog form into magazine form, like you always wanted. You *did* it."

In that moment, it was like the past few months fell away, and I felt complete. She was right: I *had* done it. Why did I keep pushing on and on, to the point of burnout, when I'd already achieved so much? What was the rush? I *deserved* a hiatus. Not the semi, half-assed hiatus I was currently on; a *real* hiatus, from *everything*. I had already laid the groundwork for this, and now, it felt like the last mindset piece fell into place. I really needed to do it.

I sat down with John, asked him to listen to me, and promptly broke down. I told him how tired I was. When I looked up, he was already nodding. He'd been able to see it before I'd even mentioned anything. I told him I was considering shelving the magazine until things shifted for me with my health and the business. He agreed that was a wise move. "You've accomplished what you wanted to and followed your gut."

Next was to speak to Chrissy, my online business manager. We talked about my situation. She knew what I was going through and agreed I needed to rein things in for a bit.

Wow. That easy, huh?

Finally, I could breathe!

Chrissy sent out an email to the writers and staff letting them know that fall's issue would be the last of the magazine, and that it would be digital only.

This was the very first time I put myself first in a professional context and prioritized my health. Insert a big sigh! Before I could fully relax, though, I needed to address my personal life and ego. Specifically, I had to confront my self-betrayal. I might have gotten my professional life back on track, but I still had a big fat Jack-shaped burden on my conscience. Over the next month, I worked with my therapist to dig into the shitshow I had brought into my space. We dissected everything. This process always really sucks. Nonetheless, as Mick Jagger preaches in my all-time favorite song, you can't always get what you want, but if you try, sometimes you might find you get what you need. I spent my days sipping the (slightly gross) kale smoothies my chef, Sam, would make me, and reconnecting with myself. Clearly, the distractions I had brought into my life were just that: distractions. Specifically, I'd been trying to distract myself from the fact that I hadn't forgiven myself yet—not for many things. Thousands, actually.

The self-healing work I did during this month, while impactful, only led to me scratching the surface of my problem. As I'd find out later (when I ended up repeating the "Jack pattern", so to speak), I still hadn't quite let go of my old belief system, nor had I let go of the story I told myself *about* myself. Because of that, God decided to send yet another test my way shortly after Jack left my life. He was on a mission to make sure I knew my own worth. But we'll get into that later. Here's the point I'm getting at: everyone—man or woman, spiritual or not—will abandon themselves when their pain becomes too much. We do this through substances, sex, work, and an array of unhealthy addictions. Instead of self-abandoning, we need to come home to ourselves and center our attention on our inner selves. We need to shed these "self-abandonment tools", clean house, and make space for ego death.

In the realm of spiritual and personal growth, ego death is a powerful and transformative experience. As the name suggests, it involves the dissolution of one's ego; the shedding of any sense of self-importance; the letting down of any barriers that separate you from others. It means letting go of your "self"—all your restrictive earthly attachments, beliefs, and biases—to make way for unprecedented spiritual growth. Carl Jung (the father of analytical psychology) was a proponent and researcher of ego death, and he suggested that ego death can lead to your integration with the "collective unconscious" (we'll talk about this further in the next chapter), which can thereby allow you to draw from universal archetypes and symbols. Other psychologists who were interested in ego death stated that ego death is always precluded by an existential crisis that forces the sufferer to "confront the void" and achieve self-understanding and enlightenment in the process.

Quite heady stuff, right?

I shed some of my ego when I admitted it was time for me to step down from some of my work commitments, and I shed even more of it when I confronted my own self-betrayal.

The ego plays a significant role in our lives, when it is permitted to. In my opinion, things become imbalanced and sinful or deadly when we allow our ego to define who we are through materialistic possessions, money, or pride. In this situation, the ego drives our desire for "more", and this perpetual desire can start to define us. On the other hand, I view a healthy, healed ego as one with a balanced yin and yang; with *qi* energy that can help *prana* energy flow through us. A healed and healthy ego is a bridge for confidence, growth, and development. Sounds great, right? That's because it is. My opinion, though, is that currently, we are all broken—*all* of us. This is a problem, because when the ego is unhealed, it becomes a liability rather than a strength. It becomes a monster that hurts others, hides our pain, and purposefully strives to drive us delulu through unhealthy outlets such as hypersexuality, addiction, and TikTok tarot readings. (I jest. Sort of.)

Over the past year (as I write), I have been in hermit mode. Like, hardcore hermit mode. (We'll explore what hermit mode is and the benefits it could bring you in Chapter 8.) The spiritual transformation and calibration that God has put me through during this lengthy stint of spiritual relaxation has turned me into a completely different person. The gifts I already had prior to this metamorphosis have seriously grown this past year, and they are really allowing me to connect with my higher self, who is classy, intelligent, confident, well-spoken, and unreactive.

So we can fully understand the ego, let's explore the biblical concept of the "fallen self", how ego-driven behaviors can lead us away from our spiritual path, and the role that humility plays in this journey. Drawing from the story of Adam and Eve, we can see how the desire for knowledge and power can lead to our egoic separation from God and those around us.

The Role of Humility and Sin

Humility is a foundational virtue in ego death and forgiveness. This is evident in the humility of Mary, or of King David in his repentance. Through these narratives, we can see how humility can lead to forgiveness, both toward oneself and others.

Humility is the grace given when you atone for your inadequacies or the sin you once thrived on. It is the grace given when you undergo ego death. Consider the Book of Job. Here, you have a man of greatness and abundance. He has everything, and, of course, he owes it all to God. Observing the fact that Job has perhaps become complacent in his good fortune, God decides to test Job's faith and humility (his ego) by allowing a serpent to destroy everything Job has. Swiftly, Job's story becomes one of sorrow and pain as he loses his entire family, farm, and everything he prides himself on. Instead of leaning into his faith and looking to God for guidance, he walks a path of victimization, not understanding why he is suddenly facing such misfortune. He had believed God wanted to give him glory.

This story made me question my own relationship with God. Was I living and breathing the Word, or was I simply "acting the part" when times happened to be sunny? (It is always powerful to push yourself to examine your relationship with God, though it can be very humbling when you realize you need to step it up.)

Sin is also a central issue in the Bible, and sin is what feeds the ego.

From the very beginning, with Adam and Eve, we see how flawed man is. This becomes a theme as the various players in the Bible struggle to trust in the Lord. In the stories of Cain and Abel and of the prodigal son, for example, we gain insights into the destructive nature of sin and how it can perpetuate the ego. Accordingly, acknowledging your own sinful tendencies is a crucial step toward ego death and forgiveness. You can even consider Jacob and Esau and the lengths Rebekah goes to in order to ensure her favorite child receives the blessing (or covenant) from his father, Isaac (the blessing was supposed to go to the first born, Esau, but through deceit, it was given to Jacob) as a great example of ego-driven behavior.

In contrast to sin, forgiveness is a divine act that transcends the ego and heals the soul. Biblical stories of forgiveness include Joseph forgiving his brothers and Jesus forgiving those who crucified him. These stories illustrate the transformative power of forgiveness and how it can free us from the shackles of ego. Drawing from the experiences of biblical figures like Moses and Saint Paul, we can see how moments of surrender and ego dissolution lead to profound spiritual awakenings. These stories serve as guiding lights for our own journeys toward elevated consciousness.

Pursuing Ego Death

To many, ego death sounds scary. It's certainly not on many people's to-do lists, probably because it's not on many people's radars, period. Sure, many Hollywood stars and corporate elites have started heading down south for ayahuasca ceremonies, but I still wouldn't exactly call this way of life "mainstream" (though it is certainly gaining traction).

If you are desiring the kind of spiritual growth that will allow you to connect to your higher self, one of the first things you should consider is what your higher self looks like, feels like, and desires out of life. These things are often readily discoverable through journaling, meditations, or help from a spiritual mentor. Once you have connected these dots, it's time to listen. This is the hard part, as most of us are really easily distracted by technology and our fast-paced lifestyle. If you *can* still your mind, though, you will be able to hear those whispers, trust me.

My great reset involved me coming home to myself. It involved me reconnecting with my higher self and welcoming her presence. Soon enough, my higher self was back to sauntering around my psyche with grace, kindness, love, and intelligence. Her gifts were now firmly in her own hands, and she had fully stepped back into her power as a high priestess. This transformation left me feeling more aligned and enlightened than ever. The ego death had been painful, but now I was on the other side of it, I was ready to dive deep into many new projects and opportunities. I began to harness the energy of Princess Diana and Audrey Hepburn (two of my energetic idols) as I welcomed wise women in this new season.

Ego death is central to the cultivation of a higher-consciousness approach to forgiveness, and the cultivation of a higher-consciousness approach to forgiveness is central to ego death. They are interrelated. Therefore, all the steps to forgiveness that we'll be talking about in this book also serve as steps to ego death. Heed the lessons herein and wave goodbye to self-abandonment.

C ONSIDER A TIME WHEN YOU were young and something horrible happened to you. How did this make you feel? I bet you were sad, and that you sought out a parent for comfort. If that little child goes to Mom or Dad for comfort, only to find their parents are emotionally unavailable in that moment, that child's needs won't be met. This (seemingly innocuous) childhood moment will then sit in the child's unconscious ready to be reenacted—meaning, when that child is hurt as an adult, that childhood moment will replay in their subconscious. This is what it means to be "triggered", and this is what Carl Jung meant by the idea of "collective unconscious". This is a theory that suggests we hold onto generational traits and memories which can filter into our current world and create archetypes (or standards) for how we show up in society.

Our capacity to be empathetic and to bring our "shadow self" (i.e., the parts of our psyche that we have repressed) to the light largely depends on our inner child wounding and whether we have healed it. The child whose emotional needs were not met effectively shoulders the responsibility of reparenting themselves in their adulthood and giving themselves the love that they missed out on in their childhood. This person must learn to accept humility, compassion for themselves, and unconditional love.

Another great theory about generational trauma was created by Dr. Gabor Maté. He explains that as an infant during World War II, his mother handed him over to a stranger to save his life. This broke the mother-son connection, which instilled trauma in him. Fast forward many decades, and you have an overachieving brilliant man who lacks the capacity to be emotionally available for his own children. --Hello me!

How could someone like Dr. Maté, me, John, or you begin to salvage the pieces of a broken relationship with their children? For starters, we'd have to own up to the reality that we have not been there for them emotionally (and that our parents were not emotionally there for us). This is hard, humbling, and heartbreaking to admit. Once you recognize this, however, you become able to forgive yourself and to ask for forgiveness from your children (and those who unintentionally neglected you). This fosters empathy and grants you and your child the opportunity to forge a plan to connect and heal the relationship.

Let's take this one step further: suppose you have an empathetic nature that allows you to understand and connect with people's struggles with forgiveness. You innately understand that forgiveness is about healing and staying connected to your higher consciousness. However, your childhood needs were not met during your early years. In this situation, your ability to be compassionate may be transformed and misconstrued, leading you to come off as cold and standoffish. In other words, you become a dismissive avoidant. Your ego stands entirely in your own way, and this manifests as you being uncommunicative and defensive; in you breadcrumbing and ghosting. This is because you were not taught how to process the complexity of humility, empathy, or forgiveness. Maybe you weren't even taught basic communication skills. Your development has been totally arrested as a result. If this is you, forgiveness may feel foreign or out of reach. That's where digging into your shadow self can help you to understand the way you operate.

As a parent who was not emotionally there for her own child and who needed to own her shit, it was important for me to say to my son, "Man, I am sorry, Evan. I know I wasn't there like I needed to be, but buddy, moving forward, I will try my best to be emotionally available for you." That's healing. That's compassionate. That's unconditional love. That's humility.

Picking Up the Pieces: Spiritual Surrender

———

A S YOU HAVE SEEN, I like to contextualize the lessons that I teach through my own life experiences—the good, the bad, and the ugly. I've found that this not only makes the lesson hit home more, but it also shows I really do practice what I preach. That in mind, in the following chapters, I'm going to drop tidbits of information about an experience I recently had that forced me to "wake up and smell the coffee", if you will (in addition to the Jack situation); to really listen to what my spirit guides were telling me to step into my power.

I alluded to this experience earlier in this book, when I said God insisted on sending me more tests so I'd finally understand my own self-worth. He sure was dead set on challenging me during this time. These were hard-fought lessons.

Please do reserve your judgment until you read this story through to its resolution. Should this trigger something within you, understand that this will be because you have some work to do in your own forgiveness journey.

It all started when I met Mark in a networking group. He was a contractor for a big corporation. More relevantly, he was married with children (and so was I), yet I couldn't deny the fact that his blue eyes and how he stood over me—all 6'2" of him—made me melt inside. We were talking business, but all I could imagine was him grabbing me by the waist and kissing me. I glanced down at his hands as I took a sip of my club soda and noted they were a working man's hands—strong, large, attractive, rough hands. I took another sip of my drink and continued to gaze into his eyes as he continued to talk about his business. I could see that he felt what I felt. We had this magnetic connection, and we both felt it trying to draw us in. Oh, how I wished he would just kiss me.

As I drove home that night, all I could think about was those hands on my body, touching me. I was craving those strong arms; for them to hold me down as we explored one another's bodies.

John was asleep when I was home, and I could hear Evan upstairs showering to his hip-hop music. I said a quick goodnight to Evan and fell asleep with a hopeless pit in my stomach. I loved my husband, but we had officially become roommates over the past year. I didn't know exactly what had made the shift happen. Maybe I was simply over his arrested development and his grouchy, aggressive Chicago voice. Maybe it was my higher self trying to shake me into realizing love is one thing and self-respect is another, and that one doesn't guarantee the other. Food for thought.

The next day rolled around, and I was in my office doing my usual routine. The house was quiet. Everyone had gone to work and school. Basically, it was just another day—until I received a text. *Ping.* I should have put my phone on "focus" mode, but alas, I didn't.

I looked down. It was from Mark.

Hmm.

I opened it and gasped. My heart raced with excitement and adrenaline.

Hello Felicity, it was great to connect with you last night. Hey, I was wondering if you would like to grab coffee one day and chat more about your business. I may have a few leads.

This sounded promising. I could always use a few leads.

As I was to later find out, the vast bulk of my initial attraction to Mark found its roots in the fact that my fifteen-year-old inner child was seeking love, validation, and attention from anywhere she could get it (much like with the Jack situation)—but more on that later.

As I contemplated Mark's invitation, I reflected on the last chapter or two of my memoir *Pieces of Me*, in which I describe the fact that John liked pieces of me, but not all of me. This still rang true. One thing was clear: I needed to really take the time to put myself back together and become the woman God intended me to be; the one who Mary vowed to stand by. But who would she be? I doodled about this in my journal. I thought I already knew the woman God wanted me to be, but it quickly became apparent that there (as always) were more layers to the onion.

I spoke to God and asked Him to allow me to fully surrender into His arms; to put me back together in His likeness and guide me down the right path. (Side note: I *was*, as it turns out, on the right path! Still, forgiveness is about surrendering to our Creator and falling into our spiritual work, so this was a necessary step.)

Something else I mentioned in *Pieces of Me* was how John seemed to fit every piece of me that I had thought I was missing. In reality (and less romantically), this feeling came from the mere fact that he was older. The wounded inner child in me had sought out a "father figure" and had, she thought, found herself a "safe man" in John. It wasn't until I did my inner child work (around the time that Mark came on the scene) that I realized I had put John on a pedestal and relied on him to fix all my brokenness. Totally unhealthy.

In a nutshell, the Mark situation was my second lightbulb moment (the first being the Jack situation).

During this period, I voiced everything that had been on my mind to John. "I thought I could trust you with all of me. You were supposed to fulfill all of me. And you didn't. Instead, the little girl in me is heartbroken, and the adult me is wicked pissed."

That was a loaded bomb. I am not sure if anyone could think of a response to it!

I took a second to stop crying and then told him I now understood that I had been unhealed when we met. "Moving forward, I will take care of and take responsibility for my inner woundedness, if you promise me you will do the same for you."

There were some definite depths to my forgiveness of John, and I reached them through various methods. Forgiveness, at its core, is an innate aspect of our humanity—we are born with the capacity to forgive—but the ego gets in the way of this.

At this point in my journey, even with all the forgiving and healing I was doing, I still felt incomplete. This was, to be blunt, a bit infuriating. Seriously, who the fuck did I need to forgive who I hadn't already? Was it the garbage man? Was it Evan's baseball coach? (Okay, so this last one wasn't far-fetched. I was constantly busting his balls. God, it's fun.) I was stuck, struggling to figure out how I could get this layer of the healing onion to fall off and reveal what lay beneath.

I was still in the midst of this mindfuckery during a beautiful sunny and warm day. I had decided to hit the hot tub that evening, and as I soaked up the warm summer dusk, I basked in the elements of nature that surrounded me: tall evergreens, grasses, the most serene landscape that the cutest landscape architect I know created for us, and a sky above radiating blue with soft hues of orange as the sun began to go down. Water is my element when it comes to my spiritual work. I am most connected to it, and typically will receive the best downloads when I am immersed in it. Therefore, it has become a habit of mine to hop in a hot bath (or, in this case, a hot tub) and talk to Mother Earth (a.k.a., my sisters) whenever I notice I am feeling stuck or heavy. (Yes, I call my evergreens, sisters, because you never really see only one evergreen planted; they hang out in tribes.) So, there I was, soaking up all the gooey energy, floating and listening to my music, when Tom Petty's song *Learning to Fly* came on. I was floating on my back staring up at the orangish sky when I heard the lyrics about learning to fly without wings. *Gosh darn it, are you kidding me?!* Total lightbulb moment. Is that what Mary Magdalene had meant in my last meditation with my shaman, when she'd mentioned I wasn't living my full truth? Had she meant that I hadn't forgiven myself? That I was still holding onto the shame, guilt, and regret I felt for the part I played in all my relationships?

Here I was, at the ripe age of forty-seven, and I was finally taking off my training wheels.

I began to cry. I felt so sorrowful for myself. I had held onto this for so long as bondage, handcuffed to old, cold pipes, waiting for someone to rescue me, when it had been me who needed to rescue me the whole time. That's what Mary had meant: I was not fully stepping into my power.

I thought of the book of Genesis, one of the greatest stories that foretells the future of Christ. Here, Abraham is told to take Isaac (his child through

Sarah) up the mountain, lay the wood down, and sacrifice him. Now, let's think about this logically: Abraham was old; Isaac was roughly in his thirties. So here, we have two grown men completely trusting the whisper of the Lord God and doing a sacrificial ritual as an offering to God. They never once questioned it.

This story, read through, is the beginning of the foretelling of God offering up His son, Christ, for us. This part of Genesis, in my opinion, is where the story of Christ really begins. Abraham fully surrenders to God's word and trusts in His plan, not thinking twice about it (and neither does Isaac). *This* is full surrender.

What does full spiritual surrender feel like? Well, for starters, it means becoming the passenger in the car. Sometimes, this feels great. Other times, I feel anxious with uncertainty. Occasionally, it feels as if my son (who's still in driver's ed) is behind the wheel, my hand gripped tight to the ceiling hand bar and my left foot on the pretend brake. Either way, I quickly figured out that we must learn to embrace this journey with excitement, gratitude, and presence.

Complete spiritual surrender is exactly what the Trinity taught us to do and is something that Christ embodied. In fact, Christ achieved the divinity of complete all-knowing—otherwise known as "hypostatic" or "gnosis"—through spiritual surrender.

What we can take away from Christ's teachings is that moving forward means letting go of the sin that someone projected onto us. It means forgiving from the heart center and letting go of the bitterness we may unintentionally hold toward Him.

God knows we are imperfect and full of flaws and that we will let Him down, and He loves us anyway. The question is, are we capable of doing the same with those who disappoint us? Can we fully step into the grace of unconditional love and spiritual surrender, for the sake of our Creator, and allow Him to lead us to his glory; to the ultimate plan of His kingdom returning?

At the end of the day, we are not judged on how much knowledge we have about His Word, but on what is held within our hearts.

Let us give the same grace to ourselves and others. We may not always know better, but if there is goodness in our hearts, let there be forgiveness.

M ARK AND I ARRANGED TO meet a week after he sent me that text. The meetup location was to be a hotel conference suite. *First red flag,* I thought. As I entered the conference room, I saw that a few other people—about ten—were all chatting and working. Mark introduced me to his team and said that his office was temporarily based here.

Okay, that made a lot more sense. Maybe not a red flag.

We walked out of the room, and as he opened the door for me, he placed his hand on the small of my back and told his team that he and I had a meeting scheduled. I felt chills run up and down my entire body. Ah, what I could do to this man. *God, give me the strength and integrity to resist.*

We grabbed coffee and moved toward the elevators. He said he had a suite-turned-office. He opened the door with his keycard, and it was precisely what he'd described: a giant suite with an office, kitchen, and dining area. The view from the window was incredible; the city skyline on this wintery day was cloudy and overcast, but still breathtaking.

An even more breathtaking sight was him. *God, he's gorgeous.* Fifty-two, tall, and fuck, those *arms.*

Stay focused, girl.

We started chatting, and at one point during our conversation, he stood right in front of me and made me stare up at him (I was sitting on a chair). We connected, eye-to-eye, for a long moment. *Oh, shit...*

He offered his hand to me, which I took. I stood up, my palm still in his. Before I knew it, we were kissing, his hands on my face. My knees physically buckled. I drew back and took a breath. "Mark, wait. What's going on?"

As he gently pushed me up against the door, staring intensely into my eyes, he said, "Your beauty, those eyes… There's an innocence about you that is so fucking sexy." He began to devour me from the neck down.

An hour passed fast. As he lay on top of me, I gently ran my fingers up and down his back to clear a bit of spiritual gunk I could feel. I could feel his energy shift and his body relax. No words spoken; just energetic healing.

It felt like lightning running through my veins when we made eye contact again. The chemistry, the connection—this magnetic connection—was insane, and what had happened was fucking incredible.

Over the following few days, I had ample time to mull over what had happened (reimagining, with pleasure, every moment). I found it interesting that at no point during or after the intimacy had it even crossed my mind that I had just sinned; that I had just cheated on my husband. There was no remorse; only a craving for more. Was this wrong? Should I feel guilt or regret? I was a little confused, and so I sought guidance from God. Still, I couldn't stay away from Mark. We scheduled a date for the following week. Little did I know that I was just looking for love in all the wrong places. This is a psychological impact of trauma, as is increased stress and anxiety, constant tension in the body, decreased emotional stability, constantly being in "fight-or-flight" mode, and, in extreme cases, posttraumatic stress disorder (PTSD). A "lesser" (but still significant) sign of trauma is subconscious deviation from your path. Sufferers of trauma also tend to seek comfort from anywhere they can get it when they're facing emotional difficulty (much like I did with both Mark and Jack).

When you become overly preoccupied with a traumatic event, you overthink, and your lack of trust and love for yourself becomes a looming cloud of negativity. That negativity takes over you spiritually and lowers your vibration, worsening any depression or unhealthy attachments you already had.

To contextualize this, let's get back to the basics of energy, physics, and matter for a brief moment, reaching back to the time of ancient Greek philosophers like Plato and Aristotle:

Our knowledge of energy and matter aligns with the spiritual principle that "like attracts like". If you vibrate high, you will attract high-vibrational people, and/or energy. If you vibrate low, you will attract low-vibrational people and energy, and you will leave your soul open for other entities or spiritual beings to take over you. You also grant the possibility of you spiraling deeper into patterns and behaviors that aren't really your own. Your vibration therefore plays a significant role in your capacity to forgive. Shamans and healers like myself can recognize when you have lost parts of your soul in this way and, if necessary, perform a soul retrieval or extraction. Here, we retrieve the soul and with love and a request for the return of clean and calibrated, high-vibrational energy. This sends the toxic entity—the lost soul—back to a place of healing love and light.

If you are to wholeheartedly forgive, you must come to a place of conscious understanding that your grudges are *yours*; that they have nothing to do with the other person. Consider the Lord's Prayer: "Forgive us for our trespasses as we forgive others for theirs." It's okay to still not trust the person who brought you heartache, and you should not blame or shame yourself for the hurt you feel, but by letting go of your grudges, you set yourself free. You become able to understand and forgive from a detached perspective. This can be thought of like a prayer: when we invite the Lord into our life through prayer, we are asking for God's aid. Similarly, when we set someone free through justice, we practice detachment; we free a harmful soul connection; we practice humility. The role of a therapist or a healer is just to hold space while someone explores their world from a more forgiving lens.

Letting go or seeking spiritual healing instead of material justice does not imply forgetting or condoning the actions that caused you pain. Instead, it means releasing the grip that your resentment has on you and letting go of any desire for revenge or retribution. It means moving forward. It means relinquishing the need to control the past or the actions of others. It means replacing the broken record of hurt and bitterness in your mind with positive thoughts of growth, so you can free yourself and heal. By surrendering your need for control and your habit of using past pains as ammo against the accuser, you free yourself from the shackles of bitterness and open yourself up to the possibility of healing and growth.

Forgiveness and spiritual healing will be really challenging for you if you think that forgiving someone is synonymous with condoning or accepting their wrongdoings (recall what we said in Chapter 2 about the widespread misuse of the word "karma" in this context). This belief can become especially prevalent when it is a narcissist you're trying to forgive, since narcissists will deny or justify their bad behavior like an eight-year-old who's been caught with his hand in the cookie jar, and there is so much "he said, she said" that the essential core of the issue begins to get misconstrued. In this situation, getting past the desire for justice or retribution is challenging. You may think that if you don't call the narcissist out on their behavior, you'll be allowing yourself to be gaslit and treated like a fool. However, the only way through this is to release your desire for justice or retribution; to allow people to operate the way they choose to, and to not take their actions personally.

I felt profoundly sad for months while I was processing my family trauma. It was utterly exhausting to acknowledge and choose to let go of the anger and resentment I felt. However, I was still ultimately able to make peace with my family and their actions through this process of detachment. It brought me emotional freedom, in general and about the specific situations I'd been trying to heal from. Now, I can honestly say that I love all my family with all my heart; they are just too toxic to have in my life. I want them to eat; just not at my table.

As you make your way toward a place of forgiveness and spiritual healing, don't be surprised if the person or people who caused the trauma or harm show no remorse for their actions. Any shock or indignation you feel about this can create an emotional barrier to forgiveness. I encourage you to push through this challenge. Remind yourself that this healing journey is about you, not them. Just because they haven't done the work and still want to operate in their world of bad habits and dysfunction doesn't mean you have to do the same.

There is no one to blame but yourself if you feel held back because you refuse to welcome forgiveness into your life. Resentment is like taking poison and waiting for the other person to die.

I do not say this to trigger feelings of shame, grief, or bitterness in you. Instead, I want this insight to urge you to set yourself free from other people's handicaps. When you do so, you not only become the master of your own healing journey, but you also become a conduit for others' healing journeys.

Understanding Your Spiritual Self

Examining yourself from an outsider's perspective—every aspect of who you are and how you were groomed into your current state—will open your eyes (and probably humble you). Try not to feel shame or guilt about what you discover during this process. Compassion is fundamental. Remember, we are simply mirrors of our environment. This process of you understanding your spiritual self starts with you recognizing that you have created a system of coping mechanisms to help you survive in an unhealthy environment. These traits might also have been modeled to you by your family. Let's say, for instance, that you have a pattern of being non-confrontational (to a fault). Where did this come from? Healthy confrontation is liberating in the fact that it can help you confidently express how you feel, in a safe space, so let's explore why you are so afraid of it. Did you grow up in a family system where instead of being taught to express how you felt as a child, you were told to muffle or repress your feelings? If so, this can result in a serious fear of confrontation. It can also lead to addiction (and other unhealthy outlets).

Identify and explore your coping mechanisms in this way, from a nonjudgmental space. Be curious about yourself. When you discover something new, take the time to process it and understand it, but don't dwell on it.

Once you have gotten a good understanding of your spiritual self, you will need to reparent your inner child and be mindful of the fact that deep-rooted spiritual healing is rarely linear. You *will* fall into old habits—it's only natural—but slowly, you will also begin to recognize yourself wanting to slip, and you will catch yourself before you do. That's the beautiful part of this journey. It will become easier and easier for you to break your unhealthy habits and replace them with healthy ones the more you do it. This is what loving yourself looks like.

Insert chills!

Too often, we aren't taught how to love ourselves. We focus so much on saying "I love you" to everybody but ourselves. The expectations placed on us about how we should fit into certain boxes or the family system are usually really inauthentic, and it is liberating to respectfully break those cycles, so that you (and future generations) can thrive.

Embracing Your Gifts

I know that the challenges in my life have served a greater purpose; that I am here to help others heal. I know this because of the powerful gifts God has given me. One of these gifts is my ability to transmute energy; another is my ability to see others' inner woundedness with just a glance.

An example of my gifts in action: I was recently at a baseball game of my son's in a beautiful South Side park in Beverly, and as I was sitting in the middle of the bleachers, I could hear and feel garbage spewing out of the mouth of the parent sitting to the right of me. My chest began to tighten from the negative chitter-chatter next to me. How could you shit-talk kids playing baseball? What came next was groundbreaking for my spiritual work: I felt the crown of my head opening and all the dark energy and negativity from that conversation being sucked through my crown chakra and pushed out, clean and vibrant, through my heart chakra. This took place over the course of fifteen minutes or so. All I did (as per the role of a healer) was hold space and do deep breathwork while this was happening. Then, the dad to the left of me mentioned that this had to be one of the most peaceful baseball games he'd ever been to. The other two people near us seconded this. I gently smiled and thanked God for my gift.

You may immediately think I was given these gifts as a blessing. I wish I had always thought this way, too. However, as a Catholic and follower of Christ, I struggled for years with my gifts. Many called them pagan, and I therefore questioned why I had been given them (and what I should do with them). For me to realize the potential that these gifts held, I had to shed the doubts I had about them. I had to recognize the fact that I would never be accepted by everyone, and that I deeply *wanted* to step out of the box of religious conformity. When I gathered enough courage to do this, I realized my gifts weren't "anti-Christian" at all. After all, the word "Christian" has "Christ" in it, and Christ was a healer. So, if you claim to be Christian, you are, in effect, claiming to be a healer. This means you, too, need to accept your suffering with gratitude (because this will spark the eternal change the world needs) and embrace your potential as a healer.

All of this starts with forgiveness.

You could even consider yourself to be a modern-day apostle. Who's to say you're not? If you are spreading the gospel, then you are doing what the apostles did, aren't you? I, for one, am a high priestess to some and an apostle to others.

Everybody is capable of energetic healing. It all relies on your desire to tap into your gift. There really is no right or wrong here; just some core aspects that we all must practice if we decide to journey down the path of becoming a healer. How can you embrace your gifts if you are not a lightworker or healer? You can practice with a healer through healing sessions. We love to teach and mentor! Consider your current situation, past experiences, and how you currently operate, and ask yourself, "Am I operating out of a place of love or fear?" If you answer "fear", then you have some exploring to do if you are to break the cycle, and a healer can help with that. Let's take your attachment style, for example (since your relationships play a *huge* role in how much negative energy is currently in your life). If your attachment style is an anxious avoidant, avoidant (dismissive), or fearful avoidant, you will lack trust, be needy, or be a runner when something challenging comes up (to provide a *very* simple summary). With a certified therapist and healer by your side, you can confront the deeper reason why you may respond to conflict like this.

Talk therapy is also abundantly helpful in getting you to understand where this may originate, such as an unhealed childhood wound or toxic cords that are yet to be cut. Once you have this knowledge, you can focus on moving past the pain and into a healthy place of openness, accountability, and love, where you detach yourself from your old patterns.

This is all achievable, no matter where you currently are in your journey.

The Magic of Self-Love

Facing all these emotions may bring a feeling of shame. Don't go there. Don't feel shameful for being vulnerable. Forgiveness involves opening yourself up to vulnerability and the possibility of being hurt again.

Fear of being emotionally exposed and reinjured can make forgiveness feel unsafe and challenging. However, if you start to reframe your vulnerability as bravery, you will be able to recognize that you are doing daring things by opening paths to forgiveness. (I may have just borrowed these words from Brené Brown's books, but she's right about being vulnerable and understanding about where shame comes from. Sorry, Brené. I give full credit to you!) Remember, you are worthy of love and should feel safe to express your vulnerability. If people do not respond to your vulnerability with love and recognition, that's on them. I learned this firsthand, through my husband.

John, historically, has struggled to acknowledge or validate my feelings. He simply wants to respond out of defense. Why is this? Because he operates from the wounded little boy he still is inside—the little boy whose trauma John still carries. John has been silenced his whole life, so his emotional intelligence is a work in progress. By God's grace, he's slowly learning and diving into his own shadow work at the age of sixty-four. This takes much strength and self-love. As I write, we are now at the point where I can simply nudge him when he doesn't validate my feelings with a quick, "Hey, John, I just told you how I feel. Can you please acknowledge and respond appropriately?"

Of course, there are some occasions when he is just not in a space to put everything to the side for my sake, and in these situations, he knows he can say, "Hey babe, I would really like to validate your feelings right now, but my mind is still processing what you just said. Can you give me a minute to collect my thoughts?"

John's family system taught him to stuff his feelings deep down, and this has rippled into self-sabotage for him in his adulthood. This makes sense. If you are always criticized, you will eventually play the part. That role fit him just fine… until he woke up. Upon me starting my work with him, he admitted that he did not feel love for himself. (Healers can tangibly feel this lack of self-love.) This recognition—that you do not love yourself—is by far one of the most pivotal moments of any healing journey, and you can transform this by seeking spiritual healing.

7
Emotional Freedom

———

OVER THE TWO MONTHS OUR affair went on for, Mark and I connected on a level that scared both him and me. We shared so many similar interests and enjoyed each other's company to an insane degree. I felt safe with him; like my playful side could come out. He loved my body, my brain, and my strength. He made me feel like the woman I wanted to be: sensual, intelligent, grounded, and graceful.

I never once felt remorse for what I was doing. The way I saw it was, I finally had what had been missing in my relationship: a connection of pure love and intimacy; a partner who always looked me in the eyes (something John rarely did).

Over time, we fell in love with one another. We would talk for hours, and we would always count down to our next conversation, like giddy teenagers. It felt like a breath of fresh air to converse with a man who did not revolve around work or his family; who did not completely ignore me when I spoke. I now had somebody who had a genuine interest in me. What's more, each time we met, our sexual chemistry intensified. We never tired of exploring one another's bodies—and holy shit, the *orgasms*. I had never had a man make love to me like he did. We were both hooked.

He dropped the first "I love you" a month or two into this affair, after an afternoon of mind-blowing intimacy. My heart sang with joy. I had felt this for a while but hadn't had the confidence to say it. I looked into his deep blue eyes and said it right back to him: "I love you, too."

We gazed at each other for what felt like an eternity. We were both lost in each other's eyes. "Felicity, you are incredibly beautiful."

We then went from meeting once a week to twice a week, and each time, we connected on a whole new emotional level. Yet not all was well in paradise. I knew that at some point, someone would have to break the ice and have a conversation about the fact that this was becoming a little sticky. We both knew how deep this was getting. We talked about the "what-ifs" of the three-year plan. This situationship had turned into a love that we both felt deeply. In the end, we concluded that we both needed space to recollect ourselves and rethink what had just happened. So, we took a bit of a "break". I had some things I needed to figure out. Was this affair my way of rebelling and seeking retribution? Was this just a cycle that was beginning to close out? I was unsure, because I hadn't yet reached true emotional freedom. I was still clinging onto another person's validation and opinions of me.

Emotional freedom is when you detach yourself from others' perspectives; when you no longer internalize what people do or say; when you break free from the confines of your emotions, unshackle yourself from turmoil, and step into a realm where your reactions are deliberate, your heart is light, and your consciousness is elevated. When you can say Fuck it!

True emotional freedom is existential bliss. It's having a best friend tell you how fucking stupid and ignorant you are and you being able to just let it wash right off you, because you understand that their opinions are on them, not you. Emotional freedom is about embracing your emotions as a colorful palette that paints the canvas of your life. Some days, the canvas may look like the Mona Lisa; other times, it may look like an authentic Picasso.

How can you get to this level of freedom?

Achieving Emotional Freedom

This journey begins with you first understanding that external influences do not define you, whether family, relationship expectations, or societal expectations. It begins with you understanding that *you* define *your* character based on the core set of values and expectations *you* have for *yourself*. After that, the five steps to true emotional freedom are 1) unpacking your emotional suitcase, 2) crafting your unique emotional style, 3) mastering the art of emotional juggling, 4) forging a solid support squad, and 5) sprinkling your journey with laughter and unconditional love. Let's explore each of these steps.

Step 1: Unpack Your Emotional Suitcase

Picture your emotions as a suitcase that's been filled over the years with joys, sorrows, triumphs, and disappointments. You've carried this suitcase through countless terrains as you've juggled your role as a daughter, sister, partner, mother, and professional. It's about time you sat down, unzipped that suitcase, and looked inside; that you acknowledged the emotions stuffed in there, including the exhilarating highs, the heart-wrenching lows, and the messy in-between feelings.

Emotional freedom begins with you mustering the courage to unpack this suitcase; to confront the emotions you've neatly tucked away; to realize that these emotions do not define you, but are simply a small part of who you are. It begins with you embracing the emotions that you discover, making peace with them, and releasing what no longer serves you. You'll be amazed at how much lighter you feel when you travel through life with more emotional awareness.

Step 2: Craft Your Emotional Style

Emotions are not just random bursts of sentiment. They are the colors that paint the canvas of your life. So, it's time to craft your emotional style, darling.

Think of your emotional style as your unique fashion sense, but for your emotions. Some days, you might feel like donning the bohemian, carefree vibe, while other days, you may be all about classic elegance. Learn to recognize which emotions resonate with your true self today and accept the days when you feel like shit. It's okay to have a bad day; the point is to not allow it to consume you.

What will make you feel genuinely good today? What kind of emotional expression will align with your values? Tailor your emotional style accordingly. Dress yourself in the emotions that reflect the authentic you. It's perfectly okay to have "casual Fridays" occasionally, but overall, make sure your emotional style truly expresses your beautiful, unique self, or the badass boss within (whichever resonates).

Step 3: Learn the Art of Emotional Juggling

Emotions are the three-ring circus of your inner world.

You may sometimes find yourself simultaneously juggling joy, sadness, and frustration (like a plate-spinner's act). This is perfectly normal, especially for us ladies going through menopause. However, true emotional freedom means mastering the art of emotional juggling. It's about recognizing that your emotions (like a juggler's plates) need attention and balance if they are to remain in motion.

Give each emotion its moment in the spotlight, acknowledge it, and then gracefully move onto the next. There's no need to drop any plates; it's all about finding balance. Juggle those emotions with finesse, and you'll discover a newfound sense of equilibrium. You'll move swiftly through the day, not allowing anything to take over you.

Step 4: Forge Your Support Squad

In this grand play we call life, we all need a stellar supporting cast. So, forge your support squad—the trusted confidants who've got your back. These people listen to your rants, laugh at your jokes, and offer a shoulder to cry on when needed. But remember, it's not just about receiving support; it's about giving it, too. Emotional freedom isn't a one-person show. Be there for your support squad, because nurturing your relationships is crucial to your emotional liberation. Furthermore, when you do seek counsel, be responsible with this and determine whether or not your go-to person is in the headspace to listen and provide support.

Step 5: Embrace Laughter and Unconditional Love

Life can be a rollercoaster ride. It throws us loops, sends us plummeting, and occasionally surprises us with breathtaking views. When the ride gets wild, there's no better response to this than a hearty laugh. Remember that you are always in the passenger seat of life (God is at the wheel) and that you always have the choice to embrace the uncertainty that comes with this as an adventure. Find humor in the chaos. Laughter is a superpower that can help you navigate even the most treacherous twists and turns. The ability to laugh at yourself is the mark of true emotional freedom (I am speaking from personal experience here).

To go with this, unconditional self-love is an often-overlooked ingredient to emotional freedom. Be your own biggest cheerleader. Understand that you are worthy of love and kindness, no matter where life's rollercoaster has brought you. Self-love is the cornerstone of emotional freedom. Treat yourself with the same compassion and love that you extend to others, and you'll find that true emotional freedom is not just attainable; it's already within you.

Maintaining Emotional Freedom

Completion of these five steps brings emotional freedom. But reaching emotional freedom isn't the end goal; *maintaining* it is. The steps toward *maintaining* emotional freedom are 1) embracing self-compassion (which involves practicing empathy, setting boundaries, and seeking support) and 2) practicing emotional detachment. These actions lay the foundation for the transformative journey of healing and forgiveness.

As you try to implement new habits and break old patterns, remember that we are born flawed. We are sinners by nature. So, we will fail many times. This is where God's grace allows us to humbly learn the lesson while still surrounded by His love.

Step 1: Rebuild Self-Compassion

Self-compassion involves treating yourself with kindness, understanding, and empathy. It requires you to give the same compassion to yourself that you would to a dear friend or loved one. It involves acknowledging that you are human and imperfect, just like the other people you may be looking to forgive, and just like most of the important players in the Bible. It involves you understanding that you were built with imperfections and embracing the humility, grace, and understanding that comes with this. Instead of dwelling on your mistakes or any self-blame or criticism, offer yourself understanding and acceptance so you can embrace your humanity and approach yourself with kindness and forgiveness.

Self-compassion is an essential aspect of rebuilding your foundation—your roots—in the larger process of forgiveness. When you extend forgiveness and compassion toward yourself and recognize the fact that your imperfections trail all the way back to your ancestral biblical roots, you learn to lean on your imperfections as opportunities for growth. You realize you can make mistakes, and that growth and learning are part of the journey.

Practicing self-compassion during the forgiveness journey involves prioritizing your wellbeing. Therefore, you should make time for mindfulness or meditation, therapy or counseling, and activities that bring you joy. You should also set boundaries with yourself and the other people in your life.

Remind yourself that you are in a transformational growth period, and regularly ask for guidance from God (or your Creator).

Understand Old Energy Will Still Pop Up

Sometimes, when we engage in self-reflection during the forgiveness journey, old energies that are still deep within us rear their ugly heads. This is okay, and is where that foundation of self-compassion comes in. Teach yourself to recognize the emotion, embrace it, and release it through breathwork. Rather than falling back into old patterns (such as criticizing yourself for your perceived shortcomings), offer yourself compassion and understand that your old patterns will resurface while you adapt to the healing process. By reframing your inner dialogue and treating yourself with empathy, you foster an environment of self-compassion that aids the forgiveness process. When they pop up in a moment, stop yourself to hold yourself accountable; after, all people will continue to test our boundaries, self-worth. It's our job to understand that we are not an option, a second thought, or not heard. If someone has entered your life and is testing you like this, send them right back out that door.

The goal is to remember that in the end, this process is about setting yourself free and understanding your own shortcomings. This can be challenging and humbling, but it ultimately makes the process less painful in the long run. It allows you to navigate the complexities of forgiveness with kindness, acceptance, and focus on personal growth and wellbeing.

Embrace the Beauty of Boundaries

"No, sorry, that does not work for me." "I have a full day, but thank you for thinking of me." That is how easy it is to begin to set healthy boundaries.

Setting healthy boundaries and prioritizing your wellbeing is essential to healing. Forgiveness does not mean allowing yourself to be continuously subjected to harmful behavior or reentering toxic relationships. Establishing healthy boundaries is an act of self-care, ensuring your emotional and physical safety while you navigate the path of forgiveness. By honoring your boundaries, you create space for healing and growth. Boundaries are about you (not anyone else).

If you have not met an energy vampire before, you are lucky. If you have not heard of energy vampires before, the concept is definitely worth looking into and learning about, so you can keep your eyes peeled and immediately see alarming behaviors and conversations for what they are. Lightworkers know that energy vampires seek them out so the vampire can take what they don't already have. They can only be repelled through firm reinforcement of boundaries.

There will always be people who try to violate your boundaries. This is because they lack respect for them. This is a toxic trait, and it's on them, not you. Firmly stand your ground and don't internalize their behavior.

Continue to Seek Support

Seeking support from trusted individuals or professionals can be vital to healing and forgiveness. Sharing your experiences and emotions with someone you trust can provide validation, guidance, and a fresh perspective. Whether through therapy, support groups, or confiding in a close friend, support offers you a valuable opportunity for you to process your emotions, gain insights, and receive guidance on healing and forgiveness.

Step 2: Practice Emotional Detachment

Another essential step toward maintaining emotional freedom is practicing detachment.

My definition of detachment involves stepping into the shoes of the person who caused you harm and seeking to understand their actions. I do this by thinking about what their emotional limitations may be. In this way, you can reach a point where you no longer take what someone does or says to you personally. Instead, you can understand the fact that everyone has limitations and that what somebody says or does to you is more about them than anything else.

For example, I was recently chatting over a glass of wine with a girlfriend, Sarah, whom I adore. Sarah can't wrap her head around my "woo-woo" world and spiritual practices. During this chat, I mentioned that I have a specific job that God has called me to do, and she responded to this with, "I don't think you are a believer or that you will be saved." I could have chosen to be super-offended by what she said, but given the circumstances (i.e., a lot of alcohol and her lack of knowledge about who will be "saved"), I instead took this as an opportunity to say it was time to go home. I admit the comment did take me aback a bit, but hey, that's her opinion. I love her regardless of her shortcomings, and I know in my heart who my Creator is and that He has gifted me as a healer to help others. Others may judge me for this, but I will not allow that to affect me. I will, however, take note of who is a true part of my tribe and who isn't, based on their words. Sarah's comment was the expression of an alcohol-induced, honest, no-holds-barred opinion of me, and considering she is a treasured girlfriend of mine, I was not offended. I still love that lady. She doesn't hold back on what she has to say, and that is a good thing.

Healthy detachment does not mean excusing others' words, actions, or opinions when they are cruel, hurtful, or unnecessary. It means gaining a broader understanding of the "why" behind them.

Detachment is a two-way road, where compassion and understanding are concerned. You must have compassion for yourself *and* the other person involved if you are to practice healthy detachment.

Detachment won't magically resolve all your problems, but a healthy perspective where you do not personalize what people think or say to you will certainly create a stable foundation.

I expected Sarah to already understand my world, which was my shortcoming. In a similar vein, I wanted John to hold himself accountable for the mistakes he'd made in our relationship, but if I'd held my breath waiting for that to happen, I would have turned blue in the face. The secret to a healthy and happier life is to build a foundation deeply rooted in spirituality and healthy detachment, with a stable spiritual community to help keep that light shining. The tribe you build from this healthy foundation will form your support system throughout the rest of your life.

8

Emerging from the Cocoon

———

THE HOLIDAYS WERE RAPIDLY APPROACHING, and I was missing Mark badly. We were still in the midst of our "break", and I was now realizing how much of a void he had filled in my life. I texted him "Merry Christmas", and days passed before he responded, very coldly. Something felt off. The new year rolled around, and what had been daily—sometimes hourly—messaging was now a faint memory. After the holiday chaos and several weeks of no contact, I reached out and asked Mark if we could speak, to which he replied, "I'm swamped."

Okay. I knew that was a big fat "no, not interested". What I didn't know was that I was still operating from my inner child—the fifteen-year-old me who wanted to cling onto anything and anyone that showed her attention—so I felt stuck to this man. Any normal adult would've gotten the hint and moved on, but not me. I was adamant about getting closure.

Another few weeks went by, and I got an occasional "I am busy, but I hope you're doing well". My intuition knew better than to let this go on, but my inner child clung on for dear life. Still, I felt used and completely blindsided. How could I have fallen for all this? After yet another cold message from Mark, I sent a very direct reply:

Mark, I am doing well, thank you. I hope you can open up and speak truthfully with me. It's okay to tell me that things got carried away and you would prefer to go our separate ways. This is confusing. Call me, please.

No response. Why couldn't he say, "Hey, I got lost and need to focus on my family"? I would respect that. This ghosting shit was insane. It was a psychopath's dream, and, in my opinion, it reeked of the power trip of a narcissist. Still, I wanted more.

I suddenly realized how empty I felt in my marriage; in myself. I had sought exterior fulfillment when I should have been looking to God.

The hollowness in my relationship with John made it challenging for me to feel fulfilled and loved. We felt like best friends and roommates, and yes, John did love me—he told me daily—but this wasn't reflected in his actions. As the bottom line, our relationship was not fulfilling. The rest of my life was, though: my career was promising, Evan was good, and I'd picked up playing the cello and dance classes. Overall, I was okay in my own skin. It was this hole in my heart—this void—that needed to be filled. But by whom?

On the days when I was alone at home, I would cry like a teenage girl. That was how much I missed Mark's connection and friendship. I knew I had a hard lesson to learn somewhere in this mess, but I still wasn't clear on it, since there had been no closure.

Then:

Hello Felicity, how are you?

The breadcrumbing began in the form of little tidbits of communication here or there. I wanted to immediately reply telling him how much I missed him, but my higher self and self-control allowed me to respond appropriately. I let a full day go by before I crafted and sent a nonchalant response:

Hi, Mark. It's nice to hear from you. Things are well.

As soon as I pressed send, I frowned. I hated playing games. And why should we? We were both adults. Quickly, I sent him another message:

Mark, I understand the distance; we got a little carried away. However, how this is being handled is a little weird to me. Is it possible to be adults here and just have a conversation?

A few minutes went by, and—*Ping.* Shit. He'd replied. I was afraid to open it, but I had to.

Felicity, I think that's a brilliant idea. Would you prefer to talk over the phone or in person?

Thank you for the swift reply, Mark. Why don't you call me when you have time?

My heart was beating rapidly. I was sweating. What would happen? What would he say?

It was then that a considerable "nudge" hit me. Why was I allowing myself to wait for a man's final say on this? *Felicity, wake the fuck up, girl! What is it that you want? Stop allowing that fifteen-year-old inner child to rule your world.* I left my office, grabbed my journal, and sat on this briefly. *What does Felicity want?* I actually couldn't remember the last time I'd asked myself this.

I made a laundry list of what I wanted in my life. It didn't include Mark, but it did include a partner with characteristics that John did not have. The funny thing is, it had taken my son's baseball coach opening my eyes to what or who I was for me to fully see this. We had been chatting about life and why it was hard to find good quality people, and I may have mentioned that men were such creeps these days. Melvin responded (and this opened my eyes) with, "Felicity, you are a high-value woman who needs a high-value man. You will not find that until you can see it within yourself." Dang, baseball dude! Thanks for the eye-opening thoughts. Clearly, I needed to sit with myself for a while and figure shit out.

I wasn't the only one coming to this realization. In a world that often celebrates "the hustle" and constant connectivity, a growing countermovement extols the virtues of solitude and self-work. This retreat into a self-imposed cocoon, also known as "hermit mode", is a deliberate choice to step away from the noise and distractions of everyday life in pursuit of self-discovery, growth, and healing. In this sacred space of solitude and introspection, individuals embark on a profound journey of transformation, emerging from their self-imposed cocoons as butterflies, reborn and ready to embrace the world anew. In this chapter, we will be exploring my secret sauce to prepare you for actual hermit mode (and yes, this did get me out of the Mark smog).

Hermit mode is a period of intentional isolation; a time when one consciously withdraws from the external world to delve deep into the internal landscape of the self. This could manifest as a physical retreat, a sabbatical from work, or just scaling back on social interactions. It's not about running away from life's challenges or responsibilities; it's about creating the conditions for meaningful self-work and personal growth.

In this metaphor, the cocoon represents the protective shell that you build around yourself during hermit mode. The cocoon provides a safe and nurturing environment for the profound changes that occur within. Just as a caterpillar encases itself in a chrysalis before emerging as a butterfly, those who embrace hermit mode cocoon themselves spiritually, so they are protected as they undergo this sacred inner transformation. This protection guides the individual toward ego death, ultimate spiritual elevation, and freedom from societal expectations and norms. It allows the individual to step into their authentic self with no regrets and to embrace the new life they've created for themselves. Embrace this time as sacred, and soon enough, you will emerge from this cocoon as an elevated version of yourself.

I absolutely love hermit mode, but then again, I am an introvert and a writer, so I guess that makes sense!

This is a journey that can take weeks, months, or even years, and it is often marked by several significant stages. It isn't dissimilar to the idea of "walking away for six months to level yourself up". This is what you do during hermit mode. During this phase, you, my friend, work on all parts of yourself, spiritually, mentally, emotionally, and physically, and emerge reborn.

Once you feel like a couple of layers of the onion have peeled off, it's time to begin emerging from the cocoon. Get yourself out there and test the waters. Are you noticing anything different with your tribe? Do you feel any triggers? Do you feel like you still fit in? As you level up, you'll begin to see people for who they are. I have been in hermit mode since 2019, and people who've known me since then find me to be unrecognizable, as I now see right through phony façades. Do not be alarmed if you find that you are not in tune with some of your normal tribe during this time. That's okay. You will learn how to be friendly with them, but with healthy boundaries in place. Those who are *really* not vibrating at your level will be plucked right out of your life (I have witnessed this on a personal level). I also recognized that I was projecting this false story onto the Marks of the world the ideal of what I saw as opposed to who the person actually was. Huge breakthrough moment. I now understood my value. Now back to my point.

Yes, you will still go to work and continue your normal routine while you are in hermit mode. Hermit mode does not mean locking yourself in a cave. The only thing that will be different is, you will start truly putting yourself first and making decisions based entirely on furthering your growth.

Let's dive into the several different stages of hermit mode:

1. Self-reflection and introspection: The initial stage of hermit mode involves a period of intense self-reflection and introspection. Without the constant distractions of the external world, you can explore your thoughts, feelings, and beliefs in depth. During this time, you may be drawn to practices such as journaling, meditation, and therapy, so you can better understand yourself.

2. Healing: Many people enter hermit mode to heal from past wounds and traumas. During this stage, you may confront painful memories and emotions you have avoided until now. You can navigate these through therapy, self-care practices, and self-compassion.

3. Reevaluation of priorities: One of the most significant benefits of hermit mode is the chance it presents for you to reevaluate your priorities. It's a time for you to ask essential questions about what truly matters in life and to let go of the things that no longer align with your values and aspirations. This stage often leads to profound shifts in life goals and purpose.

4. Personal growth: As you work on yourself during hermit mode, you will probably experience significant personal growth. You may acquire new skills, expand your knowledge, and develop deeper self-awareness.

5.   Rediscovering passions: Hermit mode often presents an opportunity for you to rediscover forgotten passions and interests. Freed from the demands of a busy life, you can rekindle your love for hobbies, art, or creative endeavors that bring you joy and fulfillment.

6.   Building inner resilience: As you confront your inner demons and overcome personal challenges during hermit mode, you build inner resilience. This newfound strength prepares you to face the external world more confidently and with equanimity.

7.   Reintegration: Emerging from the cocoon after hermit mode is a delicate reintegration process. It involves reconnecting with the external world, reestablishing social connections, and applying the lessons learned during the period of solitude. This stage requires care. It is when you are likeliest to fall back into old patterns and distractions.

8.   Sharing wisdom: Those who have undergone hermit mode often feel compelled to share their wisdom and experiences. They become a source of inspiration and guidance for those on similar journeys of self-discovery and transformation.

Step (7) can be especially challenging. It can be disorienting to reenter a world that may not have changed as much as you have. You may experience resistance from friends and family who don't understand why you suddenly needed so much solitude and self-work. Besides, the external world can be overwhelming in its own right. You must learn to balance your newfound insights and priorities with the demands of daily life.

Despite the challenges you may face, the rewards you reap from the work you do in the cocoon are immeasurable. Many who have newly emerged from hermit mode report a profound sense of clarity, purpose, and inner peace. They have a deeper connection with themselves and a greater capacity for empathy for others. Their relationships improve and they become more equipped to navigate life's challenges with resilience and grace.

There is no one-size-fits-all approach to hermit mode. Some may find solace and growth in a shorter period of solitude, while others may need more extended retreats. The key is to listen to your inner wisdom and intuition, so you can figure out when the time is right to enter and exit the cocoon.

In a world that often values external achievements and superficial success, the transformative power of hermit mode is a reminder of the importance of inner work and self-discovery. It is a testament to the human capacity for growth, healing, and evolution, when we are given the time and space to flourish.

I T WAS THE DAY MARK and I had scheduled our chat for. I was busy packing up magazines for customers and had, as usual, many other things to do. At 1PM, my phone rang, and everything else around me went silent. I grabbed my phone, entered my meditation room, and shut the door. "Hello. This is Felicity."

"Felicity, this is Mark. How are you?"

"Mark. I am doing great. And you?"

"Busy, as usual"—insert an eyeroll on my end—"but hanging in there."

"Well, that's life, kid. If we could move past the fluff talk, Mark, and get right to the point?"

He hesitated and cleared his throat. "Okay, I see. What would you think, Felicity, if I said I love you? What would you say if I said it's right person, wrong time?"

My heart was pounding. What the fuck was he trying to get at?

"Felicity, I have fallen in love with you, and I am doing everything to not just file for divorce."

Melodramatic, much? "Look, Mark, I understand how you feel. However, in my world, when someone respects or, in this case, loves someone, they at least fucking communicate it. Do me a favor and lose my number and move on. Goodbye."

Insert closure!

A lot had happened over these short few months, so, as the dust settled, as did my loneliness and isolation. The post-holidays period in the Midwest can feel and look bleak at the best of times. I tried my best to function, but the need to isolate and hibernate was intense. So, I went back to my bedroom to soul search. I wondered what God or my spirit team was testing me on; what lessons I needed to learn from this period. I dug into a lot of scripture and my spirit. I tapped into that inner fifteen-year-old who was yearning for love and companionship. I had to hold space for her as she healed from her heartbreak. She desperately wanted to reach out to Mark, so I deleted all his contact information and reassured her that we wouldn't chase icky men anymore. We wanted someone to see the value we had within; the light we emitted; the unconditional love we shared; the patience we had.

There was also still a question that needed to be answered: did this mean my relationship with John was nearing its expiration date? My memory returned to a recent family event. It had been John's son's engagement party, and as we'd walked back into our home when the party was over, my guides had told me, "Your job is done here." I felt that where my spiritual timeline was concerned, they were right: my job *was* done here. On my personal timeline, I wasn't quite there yet.

One day rolled into another, and I constantly awaited the spurts of dopamine I had become so accustomed to, and I could see now how I had been distracting myself with them. I pushed myself to exercise and do my normal routine, but the emptiness in my heart persisted. I prayed to God and established a great routine of intimate conversation with the Lord. I started to open my eyes to the gratitude available in the moment and uncover an appreciation for who and where I was. Still, I had a long way to go. I was yet to undergo a spiritual awakening.

A spiritual awakening is a profound transformational experience that often shakes the very foundations of one's beliefs and values. After such a significant shift in consciousness, individuals often find themselves on a quest to discover their purpose in a world that appears to be fractured and in need of healing. This journey of self-discovery and purpose-seeking is a deeply personal and sometimes challenging process. If you find yourself on this path after you have actioned everything else we've spoken about in this book, take your time with this process. You are probably receiving a calling from your higher self—a calling to do something on a more spiritual level—and this needs to be handled with delicacy.

It took me years to finally figure out my calling, and I had to do way more healing before I could step into my higher purpose as a healer. This is why God puts those who are meant to do something great on the hardest journeys. These tribulations are meant to strengthen your resilience, grow your faith in the Lord, and increase your trust in the unknown.

If you ask God for guidance, you shall receive it, though do be warned that you may not receive it in the way you intended to. To ease the difficulty of this process, connect with like-minded individuals who share your passion for making a difference. Collaborating with others can increase your impact and provide a supportive community for you to find solace in during your purpose-seeking journey.

Listening to Your Calling

The world we live in today presents numerous challenges, from social injustices to wars. As crazy as this may sound, I think we are witnessing something amazing. We are watching biblical prophecies unfold. Yes, these tragedies call for serious contemplation and action, but as a healer and lightworker, I can reassure you that if we trust in the Word and have undeniable faith and love for our Creator, either His kingdom will come and reign here, or we will ultimately find ourselves up there with Him and eternal peace.

If you are to find your calling, you need global awareness. So, stay informed about the issues affecting the world. Understanding the challenges that exist right now is crucial if you are to identify where your passions and purpose intersect with the world's needs.

I feel like I have a calling to be a warrior of Christ. I desired a tattoo of the cross on my right wrist for this purpose. Maybe that's my inner Joan of Arc coming out!

God doesn't put anyone on a mission without building them into something incredible first. Be prepared for your journey of obstacles and challenges and embrace it as an opportunity for growth, and you are golden.

This was one thing I did not do, and I wish I had learned this much earlier in my journey.

Make sure you are practicing mindfulness techniques to keep you grounded physically and emotionally. Getting out into nature is one of the best ways to do so, in preparation for the time when you will need to answer to your calling. Embracing the unknown after an awakening or calling can be a journey in itself. There were times I felt like Denzel Washington in *The Book of Eli*. It was just me and Armageddon, and the journey was hard, long, and dark (but worth it).

Finding your purpose after a spiritual awakening requires deep self-reflection, a willingness to adapt, and a commitment to making a positive impact. As you navigate this path, remember that your purpose is not separate from the world's healing, but an integral part of it. By aligning your awakened self with your unique gifts and the world's needs, you can become a beacon of light and contribute to the collective effort to mend our fractured world. Embrace the journey, for in doing so, you will find not only your purpose, but also your place in the grand tapestry of existence.

One thing I have realized during my journey is that we are given so many choices. We can decide to sit and dwell in our misery and pain, or we can choose to overcome, grow, and learn through it and use it for our purpose. Take my story, for example. My life has been forty-five-plus years of immense emotional pain, some parts mental and some physical, and if I had not quickly realized that there was a deeper "why" to my life, I wouldn't be where I am today, teaching and mentoring people on this subject of forgiveness and spirituality. God put me on a long path of pain so I could do my healing work and teach others what's on the other side of that pain.

I am exhausted from the process. I won't blow smoke up anybody's ass: I am one tired woman. However, He's given me so much wisdom, grace, knowledge, and discernment that has allowed me to grow into the person I am today. So, all I can do is give thanks for all of it and praise Him for pushing me when I wanted to give up. After all, I did not have a cheerleader or a coach to turn to in the early formative years of my journey. It was just me and God; just one hundred percent blind faith.

I want you to think about your journey. What role is your Creator trying to grow you into? What are you meant to learn? Who are you to become? What is your calling?

My Final Lesson

It was a sunny day in February a month or so after the Mark shitshow, and I was curled up in my chair when the sun streamed in, shining on me and warming the side of my face. I had just begun to journal a few things, and I'd just had a realization. The previous six months or so had featured a lot of obstacles, but by walking away from Mark and recognizing my desires for love and distraction for what they were, I had truly chosen myself for the very first time. At the age of forty-seven, I had finally chosen me and walked away and will choose to walk away from a few others down the road. My fantasy of who they once were no longer existed; it was the discernment that helped my judgment. Until that point, my fifteen-year-old inner child had been clinging onto anything that gave her attention, even if it meant she would always be second best. I made her my first choice when I chose to walk from Mark.

This was a huge milestone moment in my life. Over the preceding twenty years, I had allowed men to walk over me, use me, abuse me, talk down to me, shame me, and not make me feel worthy of their love or respect. I needed to start afresh with a new story, and that began here.

I started by vowing that I would put myself first and not do anything that would push my boundaries, nor would I surround myself with people who did not have true unconditional love for me.

I also distanced myself from John. I started to plant tiny seeds that our time together was ending. I poured myself into my work and therapy, exploring who Felicity was and what her truth was. In the process, I discovered that I was a mother and a wife and a powerful conduit of light healing. I also discovered that the warrior in me no longer needed to fight. She was now the empress , High Priestess who could sit on her throne and attract what she needed. She was still fragile inside, but she could also emit pure love to others.

I learned that we constantly evolve, even when we think we know the truth about who we are and what we are meant to do in this lifetime. For me, this last season was one big giant test; a cycle closing out (as I had suspected).

What waits for me only God knows. What I do know is that no matter how much somebody hurts me, their actions are a reflection of *their* pain and suffering, and my job is to transmute that into power for myself. To hold a grudge is to hold onto grief, and this will only cause eternal pain and illness.

I have forgiven John for everything in our relationship. He is my best friend, and he has offered me a love that is special. Still, it's time for me to make peace and set him free. John is deserving of a woman who seeks the same things he does—of a good final chapter to his life—and I cannot provide him with that. I want a family. I want pure, authentic love from a soul that can relate to my journey. I want someone I can grow with.

No one is perfect. Only God can claim that title. What we *can* claim is, regardless of how we show up and operate in this world, God will still love us unconditionally. Regardless of how hard you trained for something and failed at it, He still loves you. He will always be there. What we can also claim is, forgiveness comes from the heart, with the intention of setting yourself free and realizing that no one is perfect. I, for one, have failed many times while seeking love and success. Each time, I have gotten back up, to pursue different goals.

The fact that there isn't one person who isn't at least partially broken, and yet God still loves us all, shows the grace He gives us even when we have nothing left.

Work to embody love and forgiveness. Learn to lean into God's understanding (and not your own). I fully lean into the Father's guidance in everything I do.

Getting Back to Basics

In this short book, I have taken you on a journey with many twists and turns, with the intention of getting you to fundamentally understand that you must get back to basics in the life you lead. Our world has become so disconnected from our humanity that we must all open our eyes and start to embrace the simple things, lest we trigger a generational cycle of dissatisfaction and *ennui*. We need to build a foundation dedicated to Christ, love, and forgiveness. We need to embrace the imperfections in our lives. We need to learn to adapt to a "less is more" approach to life. We need to get outside and connect with Mother Earth, and give her thanks and grace for the beauty and healing energy she provides.

It's time to allow the masculine to heal and the feminine to rise into her authentic, healed beauty. It's time to create a harmonious world that allows for freedom and choice. It's time for a return to integrity and ethics; for a society where decisions are based on morality and not control.

When we get back to basics, we become able to safely embrace everyone, regardless of race, gender, and sexuality. We become able to unconditionally love and welcome all into our hearts, breaking bread on Sundays with whomever is at our front door and giving grace on the Sabbath as we remember that we are all interconnected as children of God.

We need to recognize that His kingdom is already here. It's in the clouds, the soil, the trees, and the animals. Get onto your knees and dig your hands into the soil that He put there during creation. That is *His* soil from *His* kingdom. Breathe that in. Feel it. Smell it. We do not have to allow man to continue to destroy what's already here. We can speak up and bring humanity back in alignment with the truth—that we no longer need to hold onto any more pain, regret, shame, or resentment.

Our Lord God, Yahweh, is a loving God. He loves you, me, and every other human being on this earth, regardless of what life they are leading. Embrace spiritual surrender and forgiveness, and you will naturally embody a higher-consciousness approach to forgiveness.

Acknowledgments

I am deeply grateful to everyone who has been a part of my healing journey. This includes Dr. Mike and the dedicated team at Total Life Chiropractic, Dr. Jessica Keating (my trusted acupuncturist and friend), Dr. Catherine Johnson (your support has been invaluable), and Dana Masset, my therapist (your guidance has been a beacon of light, helping me connect with the high priestess within me).

Rebecca Perry: you will always hold a unique space in my heart.

John: I want to express my deep love for you. You are the foundation of our relationship. We may not have mastered the art of a "perfect marriage", but we can always see through any pretense. Our relationship is special because it's not perfect. That's what makes it uniquely ours. You will always be my family.

Evan, my all-star. Boy, we have had many ups and downs. We are too much alike! I love your tenacity, emotional intelligence, and passion for following through on your dreams. Hon, I hope you realize that everything that I have created has been for you. I want you to see that we have limitless potential. Keep aiming for the stars, kid. I know one day I will watch you play professional baseball. I love you more than you can imagine.

About the Author

Felicity Nicole is an author, speaker, and coach, as well as the creator and owner of *She Is You,* a brand for midlife women seeking transformation and healing through a community of togetherness. Her second book, *Pieces of Me,* is a stunning memoir chronicling her life, from growing up in a dysfunctional family, to finding herself married to an abusive husband as an adult, to gathering the strength to start over and pursue something more. Now a thought leader for other midlife women who have found themselves in similar situations, her passion project, *Sisterhood of Midlife Warriors,* is a program for women seeking healing in a group setting.

In her free time, Felicity hunkers down with her family, plays the cello, gardens, and reads.

www.ingramcontent.com/pod-product-compliance
Lightning Source LLC
Chambersburg PA
CBHW021159090426
42740CB00008B/1151